I want to shout and stamp about!

Poems About Being Angry

By **Tony Mitton**

With illustrations
by **Mike Gordon**

HODDER
Wayland

An imprint of Hodder Children's Books

Text copyright © Tony Mitton 2000

Editor: Sarah Doughty
Designer: Sarah Massini

Published in 2000 by
Hodder Wayland, an imprint of
Hodder Children's Books

A Cataloguing record for this book is available
from the British Library

ISBN 0 7502 2796 6

Printed and bound in Hong Kong by Wing King Tong

Hodder Children's Books
A division of Hodder Headline Ltd
338 Euston Road, London NW1 3BH

**Most of the illustrations
in this book were first used
in the title 'I Feel Angry'
by Brian Moses
(Hodder Wayland, 1994).**

Contents

I'm angry, I'm angry,

I just can't keep it in.

I want to shout

and stamp about.

I'm going to burst my skin.

My temper's really rising.

It's getting to the top.

I feel so bad,

so mean and mad,

I think I'm going to **POP**!

I'm angry

Live volcano

The fierce and fiery feelings
are bubbling in my head.
I feel them rise behind my eyes.
My face is going red.

I'm like a live volcano
with lava on the bubble.
Oh, here we go, I'm going to blow. . .
And then there will be trouble.

My temper is a snoozing bull
so do not give its tail a pull.

For once that raging bull's awake
all kinds of things begin to break.

So do not start your mockery
or it might smash the crockery.

Raging bull

I know

a rhino.

His nostrils puff and snort.

I know

a rhino.

Says things he never ought.

I know

a rhino.

I shouldn't let him out.

But when I do

the air turns blue

when he starts to **SHOUT**.

Snorting rhino

Stamping mad

I'm so mad

I'm going to… STAMP!

And smash the floor!

Mummy, Mummy,

HELP!

My feet are sore…

Take care,

watch out

When I'm cross I stomp around.

I scowl and make a growling sound.

When I'm cross, take care, watch out!

I start to chuck my toys about.

Waah! Waah! I went too far,

I broke my very favourite car!

9

Little brother

Listen, little brother,
this is **my** stuff.
So just leave it tidy
or I'll have to get tough.

Mind what you fiddle with
and don't be a pain,
or I'll never, ever, ever, **EVER**
talk to you again!

All knotted up

Could I skip like Susie?

Could I do it? Nope!

I caught my foot and tumbled over.

Then I felt a dope.

Susie tried to help me,

but I got cross and hot.

I yelled at her, then snatched the rope

and tied it in a knot!

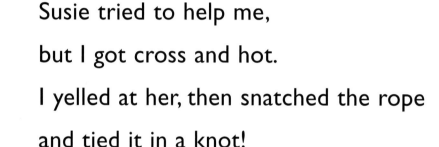

Noisy

When Dad turned on the telly
the cat began to miaow.
The dog woke up and started barking:
Bow! Wow! Wow!

My sister blew her trumpet
while I banged on my drum.
But noisiest of everything,
"**QUIET!**" yelled Mum.

Do we care?

See if **we** care.

See if **we** care.

Just because it's your ball
and you won't share.

You're no good at football,
you'd never score a goal.
So take your smelly football
and dig yourself a hole!

Bad loser

I bet you cheat.

I bet you cheat.

You always win

and you never get beat.

I always lose.

I never win.

So I just want to chuck

this game in the bin.

Teacher's temper

Teacher's getting angry.

She's got that teacher stare.

But all I did was put some paint

in Lucy's silly hair.

Teacher's getting crosser.

She's got that stony face.

Any minute now I'll hear it:

"Get back in your place!"

The cross kick

I felt I'd like
to kick someone.

I kicked a ball instead.

I kicked a ball
against a tree.

But then the ball
bounced back at me…

and bumped me on the head.

Count to ten

1, 2,

I'm cross with you.

3, 4,

I feel like war

5, 6,

with thumps and kicks

7, 8,

but wait, wait…

9, 10,

we're friends again.

Soothe your temper, smooth your frown.

Counting helps to calm you down.

Tell your troubles

If you've got a problem
and you think you're going mad,
tell it to a friend
then it's not so bad.

Something nice

When you're feeling hot and grumpy
think of something nice,
like summer breeze in leafy trees
or cooling drinks with ice.

Or pillow clouds in peaceful skies
that drift across the day.
Then put your temper on a cloud
and let it float away.

The shout breaks out

My temper's trying to trap me.

I will not let it win.

I'll try to think of something funny,

then sit back and grin.

I'll try to keep my temper

by counting up to ten.

That's good, I'm feeling calmer.

Oh, here it comes again...

My temper's really tempting me

to flip and let it out.

I'll show who's boss, I won't get cross.

Oh, no! Here comes a... **SHOUT**!

Index of first lines

About Tony Mitton

Tony Mitton lives in a small house in Cambridge with his wife, two children and a cat called Tiggy. He used to teach in  primary schools as well as write poems and stories for children. But now he mostly writes and only visits schools to perform and talk about his work. Tony says "I often get cross and grumpy, more with things than with people. Then I say things I shouldn't but mostly when there's no one around to hear me. The best way I know to calm down is to sit still, breathe steadily and let my thoughts go."